Painting on China

Marie-Thérèse Masias   Agnès Pinhas-Massin

ARCO PUBLISHING, INC.
215 Park Avenue South, New York, NY 10003

Agnès Pinhas. Moustached face.

Acknowledgments

The authors wish to record their warmest gratitude to all those whose assistance has made this book possible: Agfa Gevaert International; Artcurial, Centre d'Art Plastique contemporain, Paris; Arcadi, Paris; M. et Mme. Arvy, Limoges; Mlle. Denise Bouquin; M. Coiffe, Ceradel, Limoges; M. Deherre, director of Manufacture Havilland, Limoges; Agence PPP, Paris, and its photographer, M. Manfred Seelow; M. Jean Pascaud, director of Porcelaines d'Art P. Pascaud, Limoges; M. Roch Popelier, porcelain painter, Limoges; Rosenthal Porzellan, Germany; Mme. Saint Marc, porcelain painter, Limoges.

Marie-Thérèse Masias teaches art education and photography in the Design department of the Lycée Experimental, Sèvres. Agnès Pinhas-Massin is a porcelain and earthenware painter from Paris and Nice, specialising in soft-fire work.

All photographs are by Marie-Thérèse Masias unless otherwise attributed.

Published 1984 by Arco Publishing, Inc.
215 Park Avenue South, New York, NY 10003
Originally published in France under the title
Peinture sur porcelaine
Copyright © 1980 Dessain et Tolra
Translated and edited by M. S. Rohan
English edition copyright
© 1982 EP Publishing Limited
Printed in Belgium by Offset Printing Van den Bossche

Library of Congress Cataloging in Publication Data
Masias, Marie-Thérèse.
  Painting on china.

  Translation of: Peinture sur porcelaine.
  1. China painting. I. Pinhas-Massin, Agnès.
II. Rohan, Michael Scott. III. Title.
NK4605.M3713 1984 - 738.1'5 - 84-2915
ISBN 0-668-06236-3 (pbk.)

Contents

Uniform for a master porcelain-maker. Engraving by Roch Popelier for Haviland, Limoges.

Earliest known sample palette for painting on soft porcelain, the work of one Taunay, inscribed 'Inventory taken this 29th August 1748 at Vincennes'. Sèvres Museum. Musées Nationaux picture.

Introduction

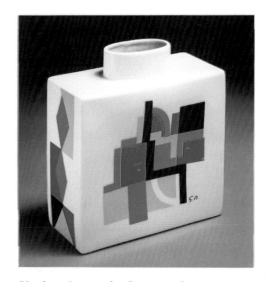

Venice. *Design by Sonia Delaunay for Artcurial Edition. Hard Limoges porcelain fired at 1400°C. Artcurial picture.*

Throughout history man has felt the need to decorate even the simplest everyday things around him. Because of this the art of painting on earthenware and porcelain has been practised in the East for over two thousand years. But today relatively few young people choose to make a career of this particular craft, because the necessarily slow rate of the painter's work makes it hard to earn a living wage; it goes directly against the productivity ethic. Openings are rare; one has to have faith, survive long periods of uncertainty, continually review one's goals. The few professionals in the field today, therefore, are usually intensely dedicated. In experiencing the deep satisfaction of creativity they are doing their best, through their medium of colour and line, to convey some degree of vision and poetry to all who contemplate their work.

Within themselves everyone has a creative urge they would like to satisfy. China painting is a form of artistic expression which, when you have mastered the technical difficulties, can give you some very rewarding results. The successful amateur is going to need care, patience, dexterity and a certain flair for colour and design.

Denise Parouty. Soft-fire design.

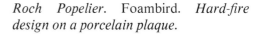

Roch Popelier. Foambird. *Hard-fire design on a porcelain plaque.*

If a china painter cannot make the things he decorates himself, he will have to make the best of whatever blank pieces he can find, enhancing them with the richness of his designs. Some ceramics craftsmen are currently developing new forms in porcelain, their studies contributing to the advancement of techniques. Let us hope that in the not too distant future the china industry will give ceramics craftsmen the chance to make their own pieces, so that these can be in perfect harmony with their designs. Starting on this rather optimistic note, this book will attempt, on the one hand, to give the newcomer to china decoration a gradual grounding, as thoroughly as possible, in soft-fire techniques, and on the other hand to encourage in him or her a creative spirit that is constantly fresh and enthusiastic—even if the first few pieces fall rather short of their creator's ambitions.

5

Decorative techniques

There are two techniques, hard-fire and soft-fire, or muffled firing.

1. Hard-fire

On porcelain

Fired at 1400°C—on unfired 'raw' glaze.

Some paint shades such as reds and pinks will not stand up to this high firing temperature, so your range of colours will be somewhat restricted. The design is painted directly onto the porous, brittle surface of the unfired glaze. This is a difficult technique which demands sound craftsmanship and a very sure hand.
Since the paint mingles more or less immediately and inextricably with its base, it cannot be retouched afterwards.
Firing completes the vitrification of object and glaze.
The design becomes part of the surface, which can give rise to some marvellous effects and an ideal unity with the object.

On earthenware

The same technique is used on earthenware, but the firing temperature varies from 750° to 1100°C, and there is the same restriction on what colours you can use.

2. Soft-fire, or muffled firing

On porcelain and earthenware

Fired at 830° on porcelain and at 730° on earthenware, on fired glaze.
The design is painted onto a smooth surface which one or two previous firings have made impenetrable.
Here, you have a wide palette of colours to choose from, and in addition the range of decorative effects possible with precious metals.
With this technique you can produce designs ranging from a sweeping sketch to very precise, detailed and even miniature designs.

Technology

Paints

Soft-fire painting is done by brush with vitrifiable paints, on smooth glazed surfaces which have been fired twice beforehand—once for the 'biscuit' and once for the glaze.
Fired in an electric kiln, the paints are transformed after cooling into a solid glassy surface.

Roch Popelier. Dark Sun. Hard-fire, on a porcelain plaque.

Agnès Pinhas. Decorative flower. Soft-fire.

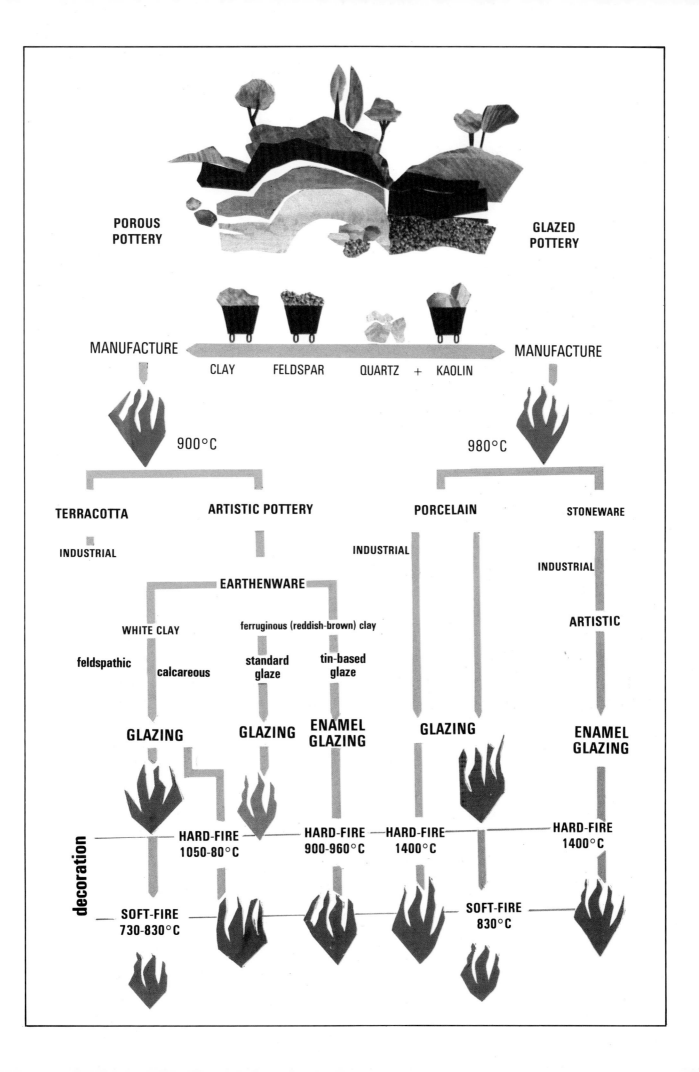

POROUS POTTERY

GLAZED POTTERY

MANUFACTURE

CLAY   FELDSPAR   QUARTZ + KAOLIN

MANUFACTURE

900°C

980°C

TERRACOTTA

ARTISTIC POTTERY

PORCELAIN

STONEWARE

INDUSTRIAL

INDUSTRIAL

INDUSTRIAL

EARTHENWARE

ARTISTIC

WHITE CLAY

ferruginous (reddish-brown) clay

feldspathic

calcareous

standard glaze

tin-based glaze

GLAZING

GLAZING

ENAMEL GLAZING

GLAZING

ENAMEL GLAZING

decoration

HARD-FIRE 1050-80°C

HARD-FIRE 900-960°C

HARD-FIRE 1400°C

HARD-FIRE 1400°C

SOFT-FIRE 730-830°C

SOFT-FIRE 830°C

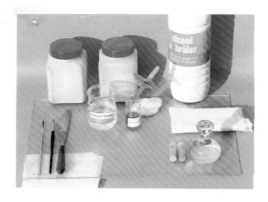

Beautiful palette of slow-fire colours made by Lacroix, a firm that has now disappeared.

In the high temperatures of the firing they combine with the glaze on porcelain, or with the tin-based glaze on earthenware. They become an integral part of the piece, entirely 'fast', although you should avoid washing decorated crockery too often; this will gradually lessen its brightness, and could eventually make the design vanish altogether.

The paints are usually sold as fine powder of more or less the right colour, but this does not always correspond to how they will look after firing. Making a sample palette or colour-chart on an earthenware or porcelain plaque, therefore, is an essential first step. You can extend this with a palette of blended colours, and, following your own tastes, another of superimposed colours. This is how the craftsman enhances his 'colour quality', which is to say the delicacy of the hues he employs, the strength or subtlety of shades or tints, and how he finds ways in which his colours may go together, and through all of this the kind of harmony which will contribute largely to the beauty of the object he decorates.

Everyone must choose their own range of colours, to suit their budget and their taste.

The range is extended by the lustres, varieties of varnish which after firing will add gloss and iridescence to the paint, and the precious metals—gold, platinum and silver.

These, usually sold in liquid form, are put on with a brush just like the paints. They can give some designs that extra touch of elegance or opulence, but you should beware of over-using them; the result will be gaudy, vulgar and very expensive.

Vitrifiable paints

Vitrifiable paints are made by combining a base and a colouring agent.

The way they are made varies with their colour—
- *mixture*, in which base and colorant are finely pulverized together;
- *fusion* of base and colorant, or of their ingredients;
- *sintering*, in which the base and colorant mix is heated almost to the point of fusing.

The base usually contains a proportion of sand (or silica), minium (red lead, lead sesquioxide) and borax (sodium borate; or crystallized boracic acid). This last gives the paints their gloss and their ability to adhere to the glaze of the china. The colorants are oxides or metallic salts which, when added to the base, develop their colours during firing. Thus chromium oxide yields the green shades, cobalt oxide the blues, iron oxide the red-browns, antimony oxide the yellows, manganese oxide the browns, and so on.

The paints are sold in several different forms, as powders, pastilles, or in pots. In the two latter cases they are ready for use.

Powdered paints

Ground very fine, these are sold in little sachets (from about 5 grams upwards), because of the tiny amount used each time, and the high cost of some colours with expensive ingredients.

The beginner can be happy with a small range of colours which he will gradually learn to use—a dozen will do. Purples and violets, difficult to use and relatively costly, can be experimented with as you progress. The paints will keep perfectly if they are stored in glass jars hermetically sealed to keep out dust and moisture.

Design by Sonia Delaunay for Artcurial Edition. Matching plates and tablecloth.

Solvents

The most important solvent for these paints is oil of turpentine (oleoresin), extracted from certain coniferous trees by nicking the trunk. This is used in two forms:

thin turps, or pure turpentine, which is used to thin the paint and which, being volatile, will evaporate.

fat oil of turpentine, an oxidized form of turpentine, which will fix the paint on the porcelain until firing, and in combing with base and colorant will heighten or lessen their sheen.

Essential oils, essence of cloves, spike lavender or aspic may be added to the paints to stop them from drying too fast. Terpineol, a liquid product of turps, is especially used in preparing white relief.

Pastilles

These are made up industrially from the more traditional powders. They are then degreased and compressed into pastille form; as such they can be used like watercolours, with water as solvent. To stop the paint running on the smooth surface of the glaze, a 50% water–alcohol mixture is much preferred.

Pots

The composition is the same as the pastilles, but sold in a paste like gouache; the paint is diluted as above.

Lustres and precious metals

Because these are all difficult to use, we believe that only the experienced amateur should employ them. They are sold as brownish solutions in tiny bottles, because they are generally used in minute quantities. A special solvent keeps them fluid and will clean them off the brush after use.

Lustres

Probably originated in China or Persia, these are made by adding metallic oxides or metals in solution to resins. Resinates of iron and uranium produce yellow lustres; resinates of vanadium, yellow and blue; of gold, blue; and of gold and silver, pinks, purples and violets.

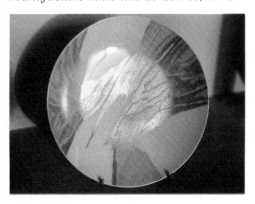

Matt gold on a Sèvres porcelain plate, decorated by James Guittet for the Manufacture nationale de Sèvres, 1970.

Precious metals

When they come out of the kiln, these are thin metallic films over the glaze. Gold is the most popular one, for its beautiful colours (ranging from yellow to green and even pink) and its decorative effects. Manufacturing these metal coatings involves many complex processes.

Brilliant golds are the cheapest, sold in a solution containing 6 to 12% gold; they are easily applied with a brush. They start off as a mixture of gold chlorosulphate, bismuth subnitrate and borax. After firing (at a maximum of 800°C for porcelain and 730°C for earthenware) they come out shining.

Matt golds

To be burnished: also a solution, of 10 to 12% gold. They come out of the kiln matt, and should be polished or burnished with an agate burnisher, a fibreglass brush or with burnishing sand.

Precipitates, obtained by the so-called 'mercury process'. These come as fine brown powders, put on with a powderer or a very fine soft brush over a special varnish moistened with fat oil and pure turps and painted on first. They can be polished in the same way as the burnished golds. Firing has to be higher than for brilliant golds unless the decoration is being put onto an already painted piece; in that case, the special varnish's flux must be softer to allow it to be fired at the same temperature as the paint.

Silver and platinum: sold the same ways as gold (except for platinum, never a liquid) and burnished like other matt metals. Both have a silver carbonate base. Platinum, being very expensive, is little used and seldom commercially available.

Bronzes are fairly rarely used in solution form; they have a semi-brilliant appearance.

Burnishing an inlaid gold pattern with an agate burnisher, Limoges.

The Haviland workshop in 1911.

Tools and materials

You will not need vast amounts of these, but they are specialized enough to warrant your special attention. Some of them you can buy, but you can give yourself the satisfaction of making the rest out of simple materials.

Things to buy

1. *Palette-knife.* Essential; you will use it to grind out the paint granules on your glass palette. For this you will need to choose one with a broad stainless-steel chamfered blade and a wooden handle.

2. *Pestle,* of ground glass, to be used like the knife but chiefly for larger quantities of paint. You will also use it for grinding your glass palette (see page 13).

3. *Pen-nibs:* drawing pens—which will need to be of the hardest steel, because porcelain surfaces wear them away quickly—to be used for line-drawings; engraving or vaccinating nibs to bring out a white streak in a block of colour, and to correct dry decoration by scraping it off.

4. *Lithographic pencil,* a wax crayon which you will use for all markings on smooth china surfaces. It looks like a black crayon or coloured pencil. Its lines have the advantage of completely disappearing during firing; its point can also be used to pick stray hairs and dust particles out of fresh artwork—no small point, as these intruders will leave unlovely and irremovable marks after firing.

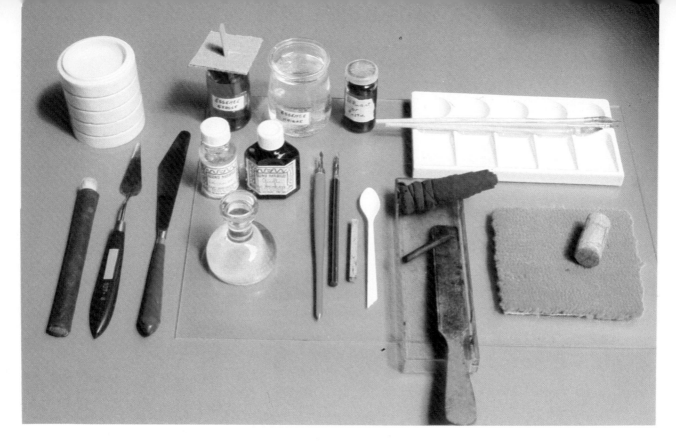

Left to right: *Stackable saucers, solvents, porcelain palette tray.* Foreground: *fibreglass brush, palette-knives, glass pestle, penholders with nibs, measuring spoons, pouncer and charcoal-scraper, pricker and pad.*

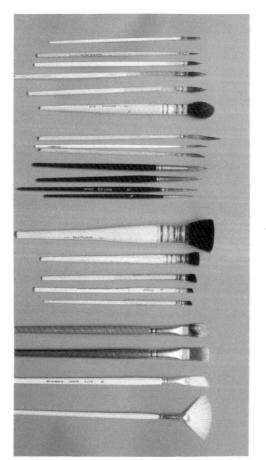

5. *Measuring spoon,* to let you measure out accurate amounts of powder for blends.

6. *Palette tray,* a practical way of keeping fresh paint. Cover it to keep dust out. You can also use a number of small china saucers.

7. *Fibreglass brush,* like a thick pencil filled with glass fibres, used for polishing gold.

8. *Brushes* must be chosen with the greatest care, because the success of your work rests quite substantially on them. Prefer ones in pen-style handles. There are many kinds you can choose, depending on the jobs you will want them for and on your own developing preferences:

paintbrushes, nos. 00 to 6:

brushes for decoration, in fine bristle or sable

brushes for fine lines, in fine bristle or sable

flat shader brush (trimmed to a slant)

cod's-tail, with long soft bristles.

Whatever you choose, go for the highest quality.

9. *Turntable.* This is for making bands (fine lines or fillets) around the piece, and any other artwork of this kind. It is a circular platform turning smoothly on its axis, on which you centre your piece. Hold your brush in a steady hand and touch the piece lightly, and the band will draw itself absolutely regularly—when you have had enough practice, that is.

Things you can make

10. *Ground-glass palette.* This is essential for preparing your paint properly. You can either have it made by a glazier or mirror-maker, or have a piece cut out and prepare the surface yourself.

11. *Pricker and pad,* for perforating pounced patterns. The pricker is a fine needle sheathed in a cork. The pad is a piece of thick light-coloured cloth.

12. *Pouncer* (a small cylindrical block of wood) and *scraper* are the tools for putting on the charcoal powder which will trace out the outline of your design through the pounced pattern (see page 28).

13. *Solvent jars.* These must all be stoppered. For fat oil of turps mount a stick in the lid, resting in the liquid, so you can lift it out sparingly. Alternatively use an eye dropper.

Turntable, called 'banding wheel' or 'whirler'.

How to grind your own glass palette. Using the glass pestle, grind in a mixture of polishing rouge and water, using a circular motion. Continue this until you begin to feel slight resistance. A touch will tell you if you have ground enough; the glass must be matt and satiny.

Cypreae vitellus, *or porcelain, the seashell whose name was borrowed—for obvious reasons—to describe a hard yet delicate and translucent ceramic. Photo by G. Salomon.*

Louis-Robert Mallet. Roots. *Soft-fire design.*

China blanks

'Blank' is ceramics jargon for any piece of porcelain or earthenware covered only with a plain white glaze. There is a wide choice of shapes and sizes, sold in two categories:

Firsts, finished and faultless pieces.

Seconds, pieces with more or less significant faults, such as black oxidation spots, missing patches in the glaze, surface extrusions or cracks, and malformations.

Beginners can make judicious use of less expensive seconds to get their hand in. But they will have to be careful in choosing plates for rim filleting, as these will have to be perfectly formed.

You can practise on earthenware tiles as well as on porcelain. The material will be interesting enough, though always less transparent and rich on earthenware.

The shape, style and material of a piece should determine its decoration. For a period-style cup, design of the appropriate period, copied or updated; a globe-shaped vase may need a curvilinear design to set off its roundness, and a tall pitcher may demand an upward-reaching design. For fine porcelain you should conceive a delicate design in translucent colours to accentuate the beauty of the material; on the other hand, everyday 'café' china will take very well to a bolder, freer design.

Your studio corner

Obviously, it would be ideal to have a proper studio. For the professional craftsman it is essential, but even the amateur needs to set aside a quiet corner—one chosen to satisfy a number of conditions the work demands.

● Choose somewhere particularly well lit.

● Keep it free from dust.

● Consider that both in preparing a design and subsequently firing it the room is going to be filled with the powerful smell of solvent vapours.

● Your kiln will need to be mounted on a metal or heavy ceramic base, some way out from the wall to allow air to circulate around it, and in a room where there is enough ventilation to carry off the surplus heat the firing creates.

● In addition to a work-table you will need a 'bench', a technical term for a short rectangular wooden board, shaped on one side. This should be put up on the wall with a strong butt-hinge at right angles to the table and at the same height, so that you can lean your elbow (right or left, for your working hand) on it, to steady your hand in difficult work. The bench should be supported by some kind of leg, fixed or foldable, depending on the space you have available.

● A drawer, to shut away your clean palette and brushes in. It can also be an invaluable aid for producing pieces in bulk. A billet of wood about 1 × 2cm and 30cm long can be jammed into the half-open drawer for about three-quarters of its length. The protruding end will hold a vase or cup you are decorating, freeing your hands and letting you rotate the piece easily without risking damage to the artwork.

● A cupboard or shelves will prove indispensable for keeping paints, solvents, blanks, work in progress and a hundred other things on.

Kilns

For the ceramic artist a kiln is absolutely essential, because heat is the magic that transforms your paints and fixes your design.

There is more than one type; you must choose yours according to the work it must do and the space available for it.

The ceramic kiln is what the professional and advanced amateur will need. As a beginner you may not be able to afford such a substantial investment, but you may be able to take your first pieces to be fired at a studio or specialized dealer's.

The enamel or test kiln is used for firing enamels onto metal. But it can also be used for firing your samples, practice pieces and small china objects. They are much easier to afford than proper ceramic kilns, but their smaller size will limit what you can achieve with them.

Loading the wood-fired kilns at the Pastaud workshop, Limoges, in 1939 for a design firing.

The ceramic kiln

These usually run on ordinary or high-voltage electric current (220 or 380 volts). The kiln consists of a large rectangular box of sheet steel with a wide hinged door in the front. In the inside the oven compartment, a proper airtight safe made of fireproof brick, keeps in the heat produced by a battery of heating elements all round the casing, including the heavy door. The case is hermetically sealed, brick against brick, to cut off all but the slightest heat loss. However, the kiln still gives off plenty of it; because of this, and its considerable weight, it must always be mounted on a metal or masonry support.

There are a number of features essential to the proper running and control of the kiln:

A peephole, right through the thickness of the door, will let you check the intensity of the heat inside and the condition of the pyrometer cones. Two or three of these are generally put in, melting at graduated temperatures, which should make it possible for you to stop the firing at the temperature chosen.

A chimney in the tip to let out solvent vapours.

A hole in the side wall to let in the pyrometer rod, with a thermocouple which will indicate the interior temperature on an outside dial.

A panel with controls, either manual or electronic and automatic, to stop and start the kiln, set for (automatic) slow-fire or high heat and for overnight firing at a gradually decreasing temperature.

Firing materials

There is a whole range of aids to firing china which will help you to get superior results by making the best use of your kiln space.

Shelves or 'bats' divide up the kiln volume into a series of vertical levels, right up to the top if necessary. They come in a variety of sizes and thicknesses—whole shelves, going right across the kiln, half-widths and so on. They are made of fireclay, lava or carborundum, all somewhat fragile. You must take care not to bang them against anything.

Props, small columns of various heights (about 30cm down to 1cm high). Some can be mounted one on top of another. Their wide adaptability makes them constantly useful; you can expect to use three or four for each shelf.

Stilts, spurs, saddles and dots are small pieces that help you to separate decorated objects from each other, or even pile them up.

Racks for plates (called a pin crank) and for tiles (tile crank) will prove indispensable when output is important. In any case they make it much easier to fit such pieces into the kiln.

Loading up the kiln

This is something worth doing carefully and systematically. The pieces should be clean and free from any marks left by fingers or paint.
Arrange your pieces into categories.
Pile your plates in the proper supports.
If necessary arrange very large plates around the sides of the kiln.
Set out all the pieces you want to fire and size them up. With a little experience you will learn to gauge by eye just how much your kiln will hold, and which position will suit which piece best.
Set up the shelves and supports in the kiln.
Arrange the pieces on them one beside the other, wasting as little space as you can. But be careful to leave a clear passage for the pyrometer rod!
If you are using pyrometer cones, prepare a support for them where they will be easily visible, and set them on it. It will be better to put in two, for finer control.
Shut the kiln.

Firing

Leave the air vents open when the firing is beginning, to let the various vapours disperse—making very sure your room is properly ventilated! Keep the kiln at low temperature for an hour: a 'soak' to burn off the fat oil.
At 250°C shut the vents, leaving a little air circulation in the chimney, and turn the heat up.

Chinese porcelain. Private collection.

Chinese porcelain, reign of Ch'ien Lung (Ch'ing dynasty).

Duration of firing depends on the size of the kiln and the amount it contains. For a kiln of about 50 litres capacity it will be about 3 to 4 hours.

Keep a very careful watch towards the end of the firing; a few minutes too long will be enough to make all your red shades disappear.

Stopping the firing

If you are using a pyrometer rod, switch off at 730°C for earthenware or 830°C for porcelain.

If you have a kiln with a fully automatic temperature control, it will shut itself off at the temperature you have chosen.

If you are using pyrometer cones, watch the positions of the cones, and switch off when you see the second one tilt over.

Unloading the kiln

This cannot be done until it has cooled completely; *never* try it above 100°C.

Test or enamelling kilns

These kilns are made of the same materials as ceramic kilns. The door may be opened from time to time during firing, which will let you follow the different stages.

They are very small-scale, and not at all expensive.

Advantages

They heat up rapidly (900°C in under an hour).

Firing is short: 3 to 4 minutes, with checks during firing.

Electricity consumption is low.

Disadvantages

You cannot fire anything at all tall in these kilns, and even plates may not fit.

Inside the kiln the oven, or muffle, is box-shaped or semi-cylindrical, a single piece of fireproof ceramic. Around this is wrapped the heating element. The space between the sheet-metal casing and the oven is filled with vermiculite, a mineral of the mica family. It is a simple, sturdy system, but its size will prove a serious limitation to the advanced amateur.

These kilns plug into an ordinary electric socket. They should be used on a fireproof base. Firing aids are simple: firing is done on a shelf of reinforced fireclay or a stainless steel grid. Long steel pincers, or a flat scoop, and a gauntlet of asbestos, or at least thick and heatproof, are essential for working with the kiln because the heat released is intense.

Shelves should be put into the kiln on three or four little supports, also of fireclay, so they can be lifted out easily.

If there is a suitable hole you can fit these kilns with a pyrometer for reading the internal temperature.

The eye can replace the pyrometer, if you learn to recognise temperatures from the colour of the kiln interior

dull red	700°C
bright red	800°C
reddish-white, incandescent	900 to 1000°C

The regulator

A little independent device fitted between the kiln and the plug or bung. During a long firing it will stop the elements overheating. It is not absolutely indispensable if the user is careful to unplug the kiln now and then.

Firing a piece

1. Evaporate away the solvents by placing the piece, on its support, into the very hot kiln several times. This will also let you raise the temperature of the piece gradually enough to lessen the risk of cracking it by heating it too quickly. For the same reason, if you have several objects to fire, warm them up on top of the kiln before exposing them to its full heat.

2. While loading in your piece, note how matt the dry artwork looks.

3. After 2 or 3 minutes, open the door at brief intervals and look at the piece, now red-hot; if the surface of the paintwork has turned glossy, take the piece out.

After everything is finally unloaded from the kiln, cover the piece with a bell-jar (a pyrex salad bowl will do) to stop it cooling too suddenly. Overfiring will impoverish the colours; repaint and refire the piece. If the colour isn't lustrous or strong enough, put it back in the kiln without any delay.

The enamelling kiln is a valuable extra for the professional as well as for an advanced amateur, because it will let him fire tests and sample palettes very quickly—and even small pieces, if urgently needed.

Milk jug, from a Limoges service of 1900. Private collection.

Learning to paint

Learning the traditional technique

Preparing the paints

This is the most important stage, because the appearance and quality of all your work are going to depend on it.

It should be done on your ground-glass palette, with the help of your palette knife and fat oil and pure turps. Wipe off knife and palette carefully before you begin, using non-fluffy rags. Dust is really the china painter's worst enemy; it mixes with the paint, or lands on a painted surface and sticks so it cannot be removed without damage. Only after firing will you notice the unlovely marks it has left in your design.

Lift a little fat oil with your knife and let a few drops slip into the paint powder on the palette.

Mix it to the consistency of a smooth paste, which should have 'body' under the knife (like toothpaste).

Squash the paint firmly under the blade with broad sweeps from left to right. Pile the mixture into a heap at the centre. Keep on doing this until you can no longer feel the grain of the powder. Some paints are grainier than others and need to be pulverised for longer, purples and violets in particular.

Add pure turps if the mixture is dry. If, on the other hand, it becomes too thin, if it 'runs' under the knife, then spread it out thinly. This will help the surplus solvent to evaporate more quickly.

Use the stick in the lid of the fat oil jar to put a very little on the palette. Lift a small drop of this and mix it with the paint.

Mix it all up vigorously. Add a little more turps if it is needed. Your paint should be smooth and fluid, but not liquid. You can use it at once, or lift it off into the little troughs in your palette tray, or into little jars, as long as these are well covered to keep out dust. Paint can be kept like that for some while, if you are careful to moisten and mix it with pure turps every day. It will only be the better to paint with.

Preparing and looking after work in progress

Clean the piece you will be painting with alcohol, and develop the habit of never touching the area you are going to be working on with your fingers.

To work on it, pick it up by the edges and rest it in the flat of your hand.

Moving around pieces you are working on is always tricky. You would do well never to make a move without thinking first, while your artwork is damp. It is not uncommon to see beautiful work ruined at the last moment by a clumsy hand.

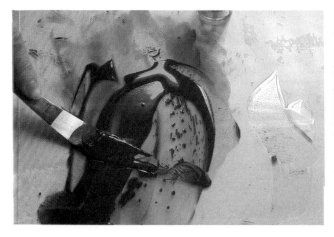

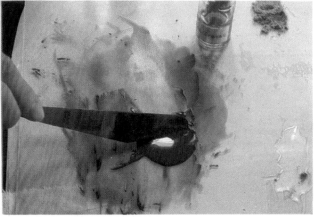

Sample palettes of pure and of blended colours.

Sample palette for lustres.

Samples of pure colours

Both beginner and professional must prepare sample palettes, on earthenware tiles or porcelain plaques, to see and appreciate how paint will look *after* firing, and so be able to plan harmonious colour schemes. Clean the plaque with alcohol. Measure (with dividers or compass) and cut out a paper circle with a diameter 1 cm wider than that of the plaque. Fold it along as many diameters as you have colours to test. Then transfer the division, using the lithographic pencil, and join them up through the centre.

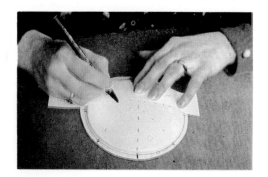

You should try each colour in three shades: deep, medium and light.

a. *Deep*

Lay the loaded brush flat, drawing out the paint freely and evening it out without worrying about going over the edge. Come back to cover the surface quickly, or it will dry. Always smooth out the paint quickly once or twice to avoid leaving bare patches.

b. *Medium*

Make it lighter, by taking less paint on the brush and by thinning it; you should already have got a lighter shade. It is a matter of keeping a constant balance between proportions of paint and of solvents.

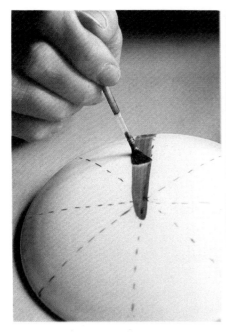

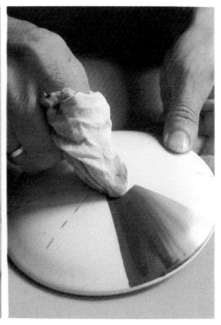

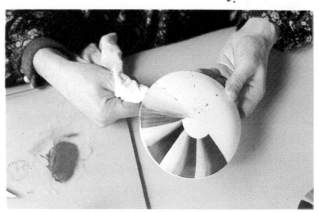

c. *Light*

Clean off your brush with pure turps, wipe it, add a little fat oil and shade the paint off as much as possible, keeping to the same stroke, right down to pure white if you can. Wipe the margins straight with a rag.

Jean Dutheil, flower painter at Limoges.

What to avoid

Paint too thick: looks just *too* shiny, and attracts dust. The design will look unclean (the paints having a tendency to blend).
Results after firing: shrinkages and flaking of the painted surface.
Paint too thin: looks too matt. Continual trouble painting and shading. Visible brushstrokes (lack of binding).
Results after firing: the paint surface looks dry and unattractive.
Paint applied too thickly: looks opaque. Difficult to shade and impossible for fine detail.
Results after firing: lack of transparency, flaking (especially of yellows), bubbles.

Simplified modern technique

Sample palette: water-based pastille paints

Base: an earthenware tile
Tools: brushes
Solvents: a jar of 50% water–alcohol mixture
        a jar of water for rinsing brushes.
Clean the tile.
Moisten all the colours with the water–alcohol mixture to soften them and make them easier to use.
Mark the tile out into strips, two boxes for each colour; one should be transparent and gradually shaded down, and the other should be thicker and more evenly painted.
Paint normally, as you would with watercolours or gouache. Use a clean brush, and begin with the very delicate pinks and reds; there is a danger they might be altered by the other colours (an important factor you must always take into consideration in your future work).
Fire it in the test kiln, evaporating off the solvents and taking it out several times to check it.

Blends

Blends of different colours always enrich your palette, both by the number of extra colours and by their added richness. You can choose these to suit yourself, but do not forget that it is usually better to introduce different hues and shades of one colour into a design than it is to add a wholly new one. As a rule any of these paints will mix well, except the reds, some of the oranges and some pinks. Only your test palette after firing will show you what incompatibilities you will have to watch out for in future work.

Techniques

Proportions: to recreate the blends you want you will have to go about these methodically.
With your measuring spoon lay out one or several spoonfuls on the glass palette, dilute them with solvents and grind them with the knife as before. Do not forget to record the proportions on the palette by the samples, with a nib.

Superimpositions

Superimposing colours in a number of firings is how a china painter will discover the unlimited possibilities in the development of his own personal palette. That is how he will perfect his technique and bring a sure refinement to his work.
Just as with blends, not every superimposition will be possible. Always rely on what your sample palettes show you after firing.

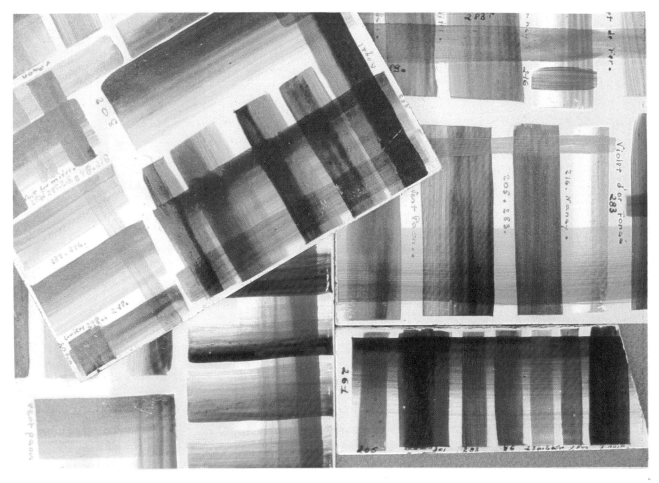

Sample palettes for mixed and blended colours.

Roch Popelier. Trio in White. *Hard-fire.*

Two or three layers are preferable to a single thick layer, which is in danger of flaking off and of looking opaque.

You can achieve:

● *a deeper colour value:* by superimposing two or three thin coats of the same colour.

● *a change of tint:* for example, by warming up a neutral grey with a yellow, or a yellow with an ochre, or by transforming a medium blue with a touch of violet.

● *transparency:* by lightly wiping over one or more layers of paint (dark over light is best) in such a way as to make the first colour, already vitrified, show through.

Techniques

Apply your paints by light dabs with a soft brush.

Fire the piece once.

Repeat the process as often as you need to to get the tint or tints you want.

Choosing and composing your designs

Designs by Denise Parouty.

Chinese porcelain plate, glazed design of the green family, showing three heroes of the epic romance Shuei-hu-chuan, *better known to British audiences as* The Water Margin. *Reign of K'ang Hsi (Ch'ing dynasty).*
Musée Guimet. Musées Nationaux picture.

As we saw in the section *China blanks* (page 14), you must adapt the decoration to the form and character of the object you choose. Whether for a simple pattern or an elaborate picture, you will need well-thought-out preliminary research—this is an important step in any designer's work. It demands imagination and sensitivity, but also an analytical turn of mind and some design ability. If, all the same, you find a lovely white expanse of china daunting because you are unsure of your own creative talents, go and look for some good sources. To begin with, copy these, to get your hand in and feed your imagination. Soon enough, you will be translating what you see into your own designs.

Starting points for your explorations might be: something in nature (flowers, trees, birds and so on); some popular motif you find on furniture, fabrics, carved wood; some colour scheme or texture drawn from a painting, or from a visit to a museum or exhibition.

In any event, you will do well to remember that design has its broad fundamental principles, and that to get the best results you should make use of these:

● Avoid too much symmetry in the motif itself, or in the way you arrange the motifs on the piece. Do not divide it into equal halves, horizontally or vertically, since a dimension repeated breeds monotony and dissipates interest.

● Make the decorated area dominant, or play about with the distribution of the designs. If you want *white* to be dominant, your motif should be small. Its interest should probably come from its fineness and delicacy. Its outline or silhouette should be carefully worked out because it will stand out strongly against the white.
If you want *colour* to be dominant, your motif should cover a large area of the piece. Some well-distributed white areas should appear in places to 'set off' the material.

● Prefer divisions into unequal numbers when distributing several designs over a space; the balance will be better.

● Take handles, spouts and rims (of plates) into account; they are all significant. It will be better to prepare for them in your design, either by *incorporating* them, taking advantage of their particular shape, or by *ignoring* them, leaving them lightly decorated or white.

● 'Centre' your pattern by eye—which is not to say lever it into the exact geometric centre of the piece, laterally or vertically; more to the place which seems to yield the best balance between design and surface.

On a particular shape, you can use a motif:

alone, if it is the right size.

repeated. You can transfer it with a tracing or a pounced pattern. You could use it as a border, high or low on the piece, in bands around it, in an arabesque, radiating from a point, on a spiral or in regular or irregular sections.

alternating: in other words, introducing a variation into a repeating pattern—a large as opposed to a small motif, light pattern opposed to dark (positive–negative, perhaps), plain area as opposed to worked, right-facing as opposed to left-facing motif.

superimposed: motifs can be juxtaposed, overlapped, fitted into each other. The distribution of colours and shades will be of great importance—it should be studied seriously. We do not have the room to give you all the essentials here, but going to specialist books on design can bring you invaluable assistance.

L.-R. Mallet. Soft-fire design. The square birds fit the shape of the piece.

Preliminary work on the piece using litho pencil. Design in lustres. Agnès Pinhas.

Planning your designs

There are a number of ways you can plan.

1. Preliminary sketches on paper and tracings

Analyse the shape of the piece, so it is clear in your mind.

Do several free sketches; then, considering the principles set out above, choose the best.

Refine and complete your design, making one or more tracings of it.

Transfer your pattern to the piece by following the lines of the tracing on its other side with lithographic pencil, then using it like carbon paper.

2. Planning directly onto the piece

Assessing the piece to be decorated *visually,* draw your design spontaneously onto it with the litho pencil. The design will 'lay itself out' better, meaning it will fit itself almost automatically to the ideal shape for the piece.

Draw freely with bold strokes.

Refine your sketch, rubbing it out with your fingertip where necessary until the design pleases you and seems to fit the form.

Look at the piece in a mirror; any mistakes in composition will seem to stand out when the image is reversed.

If your drawing is too laboured, you risk making the surface of the piece greasy. You should then take tracings of the design, marking location points so you can align the tracing exactly as before.

Clean the piece off completely with alcohol and dry it.

Align the tracing and hold it in place with sellotape.

Transfer the design by drawing along the lines with a hard well-sharpened pencil.

Transferring a design

Pouncing

This is a handy way of transferring a design. It is done with a design drawn on tracing paper and then pricked through with the needle along all the lines at regular 2mm intervals. Charcoal dust smeared on the pattern marks it out in dots on the piece. A pounced pattern has many advantages: it is easy to make (though finicky), and transfers quickly and accurately. It lets you use the same motif repeatedly and allows the uncertain painter to work on a clear, unproblematical design (easy to erase and to restore if you make a mistake).

Procedure

Choose the sketch that is most interesting and rework it full size, using successive sketches until your design is absolutely complete. Use this last tracing for pouncing.

Rest it on a small pad of soft cloth. Prick it cleanly along the pencil lines at regular 2mm intervals.

When you have finished this, turn the tracing over and rub the lines very gently with extremely fine glasspaper to clean off shreds around the holes; this will open them up to let the powder through neatly.

Rub the pouncer over the charcoal grater.

Steady the tracing on the piece.

Rub the pouncer across it in swirls to lay down the charcoal on the piece.

Pieces with difficult shapes

On such a piece (which should encourage you to draw the design on directly) the tracing will be harder to manage; to reconcile it with the shape and avoid handles, spouts, fluting and so on, you will need to break it up into as many separate sheets as are needed to cover the space. You can use dividers to mark out suitable divisions (see page 22); the procedure is the same for the height of the piece. Mark out corresponding generative lines; cut out several pieces of tracing paper in the shape of the various divisions and copy the appropriate parts of the pattern onto them. Number each piece.

Developing essential skills

In the remaining chapters are a series of simple exercises which, if worked through progressively, should leave you with a reasonable command of the necessary skills. You will be well advised, if you want to avoid more than your share of setbacks and disappointments, to follow our instructions closely. In particular, follow all of them concerning the preparation of your work, because you should begin to develop good working habits right from the beginning. In the chapters that follow, those instructions are taken as read.

First designs for single firing

Butterflies

These two exercises will give beginners a chance to practise the proper preparation of their paints.

Choose a small and more-or-less flat blank to decorate, perhaps an earthenware tile or a porcelain ashtray.

Clean the piece with alcohol.

Choose a fine paintbrush.

Select colours that are easy to work with (no pinks or violets) and prepare them as for the sample palette.

Design by Agnès Pinhas.

Single colour

Make a pounced pattern of your design, and transfer it.

Load the brush with paint; stroke it gently against the glass palette to remove any excess and shape its point.

Apply the paint carefully.

If you make a mistake, wipe it out with a rag if necessary.

Keep work in progress out of the way of dust—you can simply turn hollow shapes like the ashtray upside down.

Four colours

You are best to begin with the colour that dominates the design, light blue in the illustration.

Tidy up the drawing, using the pointed tip of the brush-handle, the ideal shape for the job.

Go on painting each colour separately.

The design must be clearly outlined; the paints must nowhere overlap or mix.

Blue horse

Water-based pastille paints

Draw and transfer the pattern.

Moisten all the pastilles with a brush to soften the paint; do not forget that reds and pinks are not to be mixed.

Apply the colours in thin coats to get a transparent effect, but in one or two small patches make it thicker, smoothing it out well, to create a pleasant contrast.

The paints dry quickly, which will allow you to add details or even another coat more or less at once, passing the brush quickly over the dry paint only once—no return strokes.

To bring out white details or highlights, you can scratch away dry paint with a nib or a pointed stick.

Firing

This can be done in the test kiln.

Refer back to the section on firing. It is important that the paint be completely dry.

Wait until no more vapour is given off.

Place the piece as deep into the kiln as you can, for better firing, and turn it round with the pincers occasionally so it will fire evenly.

Watch for the moment when the paint begins to become glossy.

Make a rest for it.

Take it out of the kiln and cover it.

Design by Marie-Thérèse Masias.

Baba

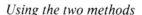

Design by Marie-Thérèse Masias.

Pen drawing

With this technique you can produce designs as spontaneous as a thumbnail sketch, or precise and crammed with detail.
For this you will need to prepare the paint a special way. One of two mixtures can be used:
—with water and powdered sugar, for a hard line;
—with fat oil and pure turps, for a softer line.

1. With water and sugar

Mix the powder with a little water, to form a paste.
Crush and squash the grains well.
Add sugar and water, and continue to reduce the powder until the sugar has dissolved.
The resulting mix should be liquid enough to flow easily off your nib.
Since the line dries very quickly on its background, you can easily scratch away any lines you want to with the scraper nib, and if necessary replace the pounced outline to have another try.

2. With turps

To get this right, follow the order of operations exactly.
Blend your powder with some pure turps, without drowning it.
Make a paste.
Mix and crush the grains well, adding a very little pure turps if needed.
Add a *very* little fat oil, then some more pure turps to stretch the mixture and bring it to the right consistency.
The line will be softer.

Using the two methods

Load your pen very lightly.
Wipe it often, or it will very soon clog up and the paint will flow badly.
Apply a regular outline first, then add thicker and thinner areas, on small surfaces. Then take some trouble to work out decorative effects to get a more refined and contrasted outline.
Clean your palette after each use; this paint cannot be kept.

Design by Marie-Thérèse Masias.

Brush lines

Working on this design, done with the brush only, will help you to develop a supple and controlled hand. It is done as a 'cameo', or single-tint drawing, using different shades of blue, light, medium and deep.

Select an artists' brush with long fine bristles.
Keep faithfully to the pattern to follow the curves and contours accurately.
Do not use too much paint at once; put little on your brush and go back often for more.
Take advantage of all the shapes your brush can take on, pressing it down for the fuller parts of the line (the troughs) and lift it to go on to the finer parts (the crests).
Work slowly and draw out your paint well.

Detail of the design by Agnès Pinhas.

Decorative flower pattern

Nib and brush

Draw the heart of the flower first.

Draw the petals, studying their shapes and profiles carefully.

Scrape out the heart pattern with the rounded end of the brush handle.

Paint the remaining petals with the brush, in three different shades.

Finish with the stalk and leaves; paint them in with light touches, then go back over them with the nib to refine the design.

Laying down a background

Some designs must have a background of solid colour.

Tools and solvents

Two sable brushes, one large, one medium.
A cod's-tail brush with soft bristles or a large artists' brush.
Oil of cloves.

Design by Marie-Thérèse Masias.

Practice on an earthenware tile

Single base colour

Prepare enough paint to cover the whole surface of the piece. Add a little oil of cloves to the mix.
If you do not have any, make up a mix with rather more fat oil than usual.
After you have painted the edges of the tile, apply the paint *quickly* with the cod's-tail brush.
Tint it, which is to say pat the painted surface all over softly but firmly with the large brush, holding it by the top of its handle, so as to achieve an even surface. Continue with the other brush. No trace of brushstrokes should remain.
Beware of dark-coloured backgrounds, which can look very beautiful but can make it hard to get the surface perfectly even.

Multicoloured backgrounds

Having prepared your paints—taking account of the possible blends and overlaps worked out on your sample palettes—apply your paints one after the other, mingling and shading them as suits you.
Tint as above.
With this technique you can create fascinating and subtle background effects.

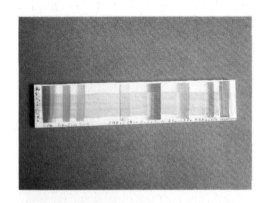

Balloon

Design in two firings

First firing

Sample the paints you are going to use.
Fire the sample.
Apply the pounced pattern to the cup.
Adjust it.
Apply the yellow ground to the cup and the rim of the saucer.
Tint if you need to, but it should not be absolutely necessary.

Second firing

Draw the detail onto the cup and saucer with a nib.
Fill in the small spots of colour.

Design by Marie-Thérèse Masias.

Special techniques

Banding

Banding can round off a pattern and enhance it—or be a pattern in itself. Using it demands some practice and plenty of dexterity: the beginner will find it difficult to align band properly. Also, on porcelain the lines must be particularly clean and precise: earthenware can stand something a little less regular.

Tools and materials

You cannot do without a stand-mounted turntable. It will be easier to adapt to the height of your bench, and so be easier to handle.

The banding brush must have enough bristles to allow the paint to flow freely, but at the same time be fine enough to paint ultra-thin 'hairline' bands.

Preparing the paint

Make a fair amount, because this technique uses a lot of paint, and to begin with you will need to practise it several times.

The mixture must be properly fluid, but neither too liquid nor too thick. We recommend you use oil of cloves for a better line.

Alignment

If the piece is so light that it may move during banding, weight it down with a stable weight.

The grooves on the turntable platter may help you get the piece in the exact centre, but they are generally not enough.

With your right arm leaning firmly on the bench, use a finger of your right hand as a gauge. Turn the platter gently with your left hand and ease the piece in or out according to the gap between it and your finger. The platter should be turned anticlockwise.

Painting the bands

Load the brush enough for it not to need reloading during the process, and check that it tapers down to a proper point.

Set the turntable moving, and rest the point of the brush against the piece, pressing progressively harder, then lifting it up at the end for a perfect join.

The turntable can be a design tool in creating modern decoration composed of irregular stripes, interspersed with drawings and splashes of colour.

It also makes an excellent support for flat pieces such as plates while you are working on them, saving your left arm from getting tired.

Stencils

Stencils are very useful decorative aids, making it possible for your to produce designs based on geometrical forms or simple outlines quickly and easily—although the final composition may be as complex as you like.

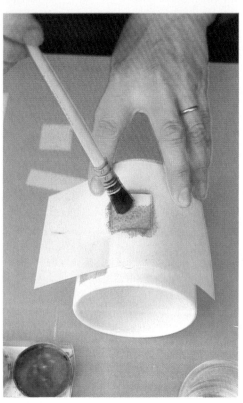

You can use the stencil two ways: with the brush and water-based colours, or with a sprayer.

1. With the brush and water-based colours, which have the advantage of drying rapidly. You can therefore apply the stencilled patterns one on top of the other, and manage superimpositions and scrapings-out without having to fire the piece between operations.
Cut out your outlines in strong tracing paper, using a craft knife.
Align the first stencil, holding it firmly in place with the right hand.
Dab on the chosen colour with the brush.
Draw out the motifs by scratching with a pointed stick.

2. With the sprayer, which can either lay down a light layer of base colour under motifs, or the motifs themselves. Sprayers are not recommended for amateur use, but if they are used the proper precautions *must* be observed—including the wearing of protective clothing and a face-mask.

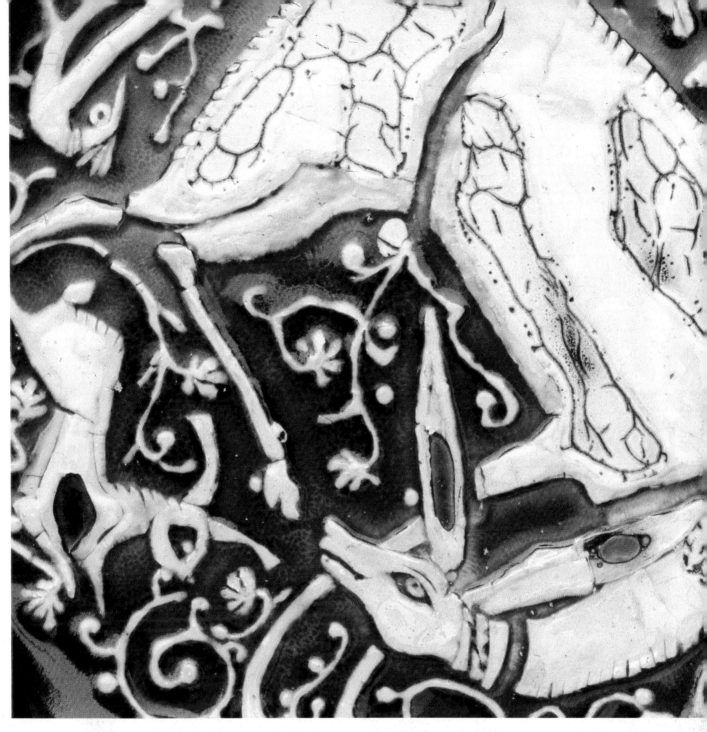

Relief, or white relief

White-relief design, in stages. An accidental effect of over-firing has been made use of to enrich the design.

As its name suggests, this paint allows you to create, with brush or dry-point, a design with detail that stands out as if sculpted, rather like a proper bas-relief.

It can be left plain white, showing off the areas of pattern and delicate details to advantage, or painted in shades of one colour, or in several colours. It is sold as a white powder, to be pulverized on the palette with knife and solvent: this is terpineol, light pine oil, which will mix up to a smooth paste, fine enough to take every delicate detail, but not runny.

This technique has been much used in China and the East generally.

Caravel

Design by Marie-Thérèse Masias.

Brush and dry-point technique

First firing

Prepare the paint only when you are ready to use it.

Load a brush, fine and soft, with the paste in the normal way, and lay it on flat at first.

Reload the brush, lay on another layer of paste, smooth it down, and continue the procedure.

Firing will be a delicate business, because if it is insufficient you will get a brittle result, a grainy relief; the result of over-high firing will be a sudden bloating of the design and consequent disappearance of the detail. Evaporating off the solvent is the most important part of the process. Avoid rushing it.

Keep an eye on the firing by opening the kiln door. The moment the surface develops a slight film and begins to look smooth, take the piece out very quickly.

Let it cool out of all draughts.

Second firing

Come back to this, following the same process, as many times as necessary to build up the relief you want.

Once the work has hardened, refine the design with the dry-point—but with a light hand, or you risk cracking away some or all of the design!

Let the crust harden for a few minutes, so you can add precise details (to the hull, the birds, and so on).

Fire the piece once more.

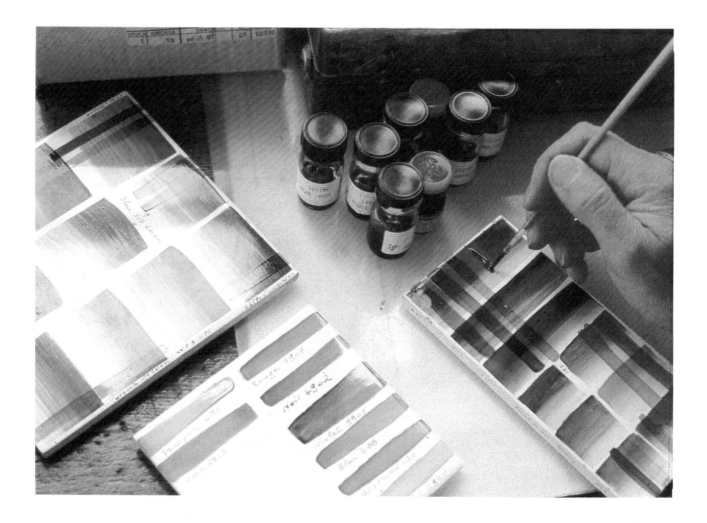

Lustres

The charming metallic sheen of lustres can bring a very delicate beauty to some designs.

1. Traditional technique

Traditionally lustres were superimposed on a painted surface that had already been fired once, to warm up a design or make a background.

2. Use in modern designs

Their iridescence may introduce many fascinating effects into a design, but use them badly and they will look vulgar and tinselly.
We can suggest two ways of using them:
● to heighten a painted design with touches of light, painted shade on shade (paint, then lustre);
● as delicate shading for a line drawing, animating it with their sparkle.
This is the way we are going to try.
You should make a sample palette before you begin, so as to become familiar with the lustres before and after firing.

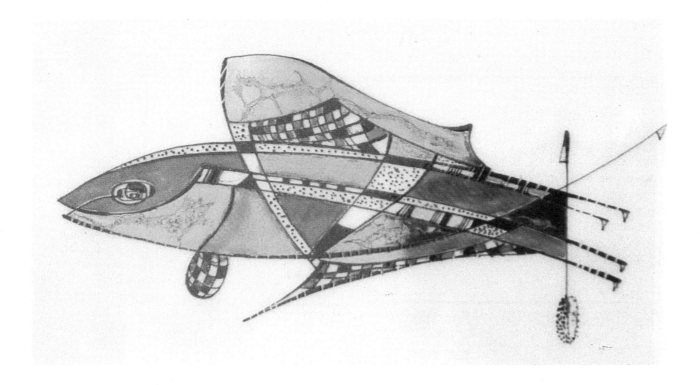

Lustre design by Agnès Pinhas.

Fish

It will be useful to find a subtle design, with room for small solid areas and light touches of three or four lustre colours, based on a black line-drawing.

Tools and materials

Brushes which will only be used for lustres.
A special solvent for gold and lustres, in which you can also clean off your brushes.
Oil of spike lavender, used chiefly for laying down ground and letting you 'stretch' your lustres.
A crackling solution for marbled effects.

Procedure

Shake the bottle of paint vigorously each time you use it. Shut it properly immediately you have finished with it.
Dip your brush directly into the liquid and lift out a very little.
Apply it as required, drawing it out well to avoid thickened areas.
Clean the brush and wipe it very carefully. An overloaded brush will increase the natural fluidity of the paint.
Completed pieces must be kept absolutely free from dust until they go into the kiln.
To obtain marbled textures, first apply a ground coat, let it dry for a few minutes, then, still with the brush, dab minute drops of crackling solution, and let it dry before firing.

Firing

This is a difficult process, which needs to be taken slowly.

In a ceramic kiln

Set the kiln to Soft-Fire.
Open the air vents or bung; humidity and solvent vapours absolutely *must* be dispersed at the beginning of firing.
Shut the vents at about 400°C.
Then set the kiln thermostat to Hard-Fire (the normal position for firing porcelain or earthenware).
Do not confuse this specific term, referring to heating rate, with the hard-fire technique, for china decoration (firing at 1400°C).
Let the temperature rise to 720°C for earthenware, 800°C for porcelain.

In the test kiln

Hold the piece at the kiln door as it heats up, with the end of your pincers, to warm it up and help the vapours evaporate.
Place it in the kiln only when it is absolutely dry.
Shut the door for a few minutes to let the temperature rise.
Then open it, to control the effect, until the paint becomes glossy; keep it in for a few minutes more to fix the material properly.

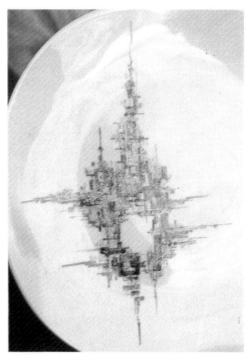

Design by L.-R. Mallet.

Ancient Gaul. *Design by L.-R. Mallet.*

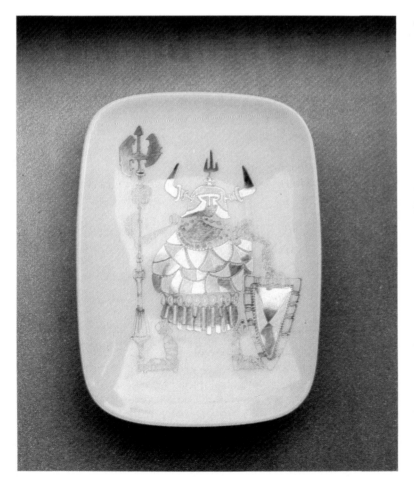

Precious metals

Gold, silver, platinum, bronze

Laying liquid gold over a painted ground.

Designs by Bjorn Wiinblad for Rosenthal Studio-Linie. Rosenthal picture.

These are essential extensions of any decorator's palette, and a valuable aid to improving your designs.

Their mode of use has remained the same from the oldest works to present-day creations.

The shiny metals are just as likely to look tinselly as the lustres; in contrast, the matt metals are always lovely, but unhappily much more troublesome.

Gold will do very well by itself, as can be seen in the contemporary work of J. Guittet for the Sèvres Manufacture.

You can also use it just as well for fillets, characters (such as initials) and also as part of decorative artwork. It then acts as a colour, can be considered as one, and should integrate itself normally into a harmonious colour scheme.

Vase of Gensoli shape. The design (no. 2259) was created by M. Ney for the Manufacture nationale de Sèvres.

Sample palette for precious metals.

Design by Agnès Pinhas.

Round fish

Black line pen drawing with small areas of matt gold.
Shake the bottle well before each use and stopper it immediately after use.
Lay down a very little gold on your glass palette, if possible with the end of the stopper.
Draw out the gold on the piece; a medium-thin coat will do, in an even layer without thick areas.

Firing

As with lustres, let the vapours burn off and evaporate completely at the beginning of firing. However, this time switch the kiln directly to Hard-Fire. Temperature: 720°C for earthenware, 800°C for porcelain.

After firing

Polishing or burnishing:
Rub the gold lightly with the fibreglass brush to bring out all its sparkle. For the best results you can use agate burnishers.
If the gold has been put on too thinly it will develop a pinkish look. In that case put on another layer and fire it again.

45

Using your skills

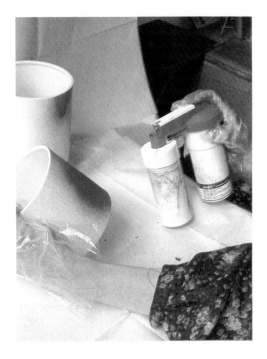

Experimenting with backgrounds and textures on a vase

A painter enjoys developing ways of artistic expression that are wholly his own, to bring out the beauty in his raw materials and make his designs stand out against a background that is rich in itself.

This exercise is to accustom us to using different tools, and to improvising others—somewhat unexpected—in order to discover new decorative effects, on the sides of a vase.

Some parts of the result are interesting, others disappointing, but it was an enriching and very entertaining experience; each of us in turn tried to outdo the other in creative imagination, dreaming up new ways of decorating the surfaces.

Some essentials

In decorating porcelain, never forget to show off its translucency; leave areas blank or use light or transparent shades.

On earthenware you can load up with rather more colour, as there is less risk of flaking than with porcelain. Remember, too, that the colours will come up brighter than on porcelain.

You will need a minimum of two firings.

The first firing will essentially provide a coloured base on which the next firing's work will be built up. The choice and placing of colours becomes very important. Some mistakes cannot be redeemed; if you forget to leave some areas white, or to provide some lighter areas, you will never get them back. You can, though, always darken and deepen an overlight base.

The second firing will give free rein to the imagination of an experienced painter—you.

But you cannot afford to lose sight of the problems of superimposing colours, so keep on referring to your sample palettes.

Free decoration on a vase

Handling the piece

See the general notes in the section on 'Your studio corner', page 15.

Moving around a piece in progress—or just completed—is rather a problem, since you will not be able to hold the vase anywhere on the outside. You will therefore have to stick your hand, or some fingers at least, into the neck of the vase, not picking it up and carrying it until you are sure of your grip.

First firing

Prepare the paint, making it very liquid so it can pass through the nozzles of the sprayer. Provide adequate protection from the spray—see page 38.

Checking the intensity of the spray on the vase, lay down a fine film of paint. Linger in places to get deeper shades, but lightly, or you will only make unsightly and irreparable runs.

Paint strips of colours that go together, in deeper and lighter shadings.

Tint if you want to (see page 35).

Scratch around with the blunt tip of the brush. Bring out background textures with a finger; and scratch with a comb.

Now carry out the first firing. The patience of the 'action painter' is sorely tested!

The second firing is going to try it further:

Work for the first firing.

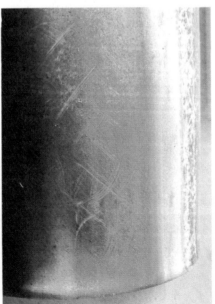

48

Second firing

Spray with the same colour as for the first firing.
Paint all around the vase.
Repaint the same light and dark tones.
Lay down warm colours to make it 'sing'.
Dab with a stiff cod's-tail brush, skimming it lightly over the surface.
Scrape at the painted areas with string to bring out a light line pattern.
Bring out the background with a finger.
Add a few pen drawings.
Sign the masterpiece!
Second firing.

Work for the second firing.

Design by Agnès Pinhas.

Bird plate

Using your experience so far.

First firing

Apply a very light ground, bringing out the textures in the background material here and there.

Second firing

Draw the lines of the bird design with a nib.
Add the various colours by brush.

Earthenware tiles

Soft-fire techniques are admirably suited to earthenware.
Firing makes the paints brighter than on porcelain, and they respond well to all the techniques we have so far covered. There are a great many ways for you to exploit these advantages, ranging from the surface of a single tile to huge compound murals (and table-mats, tile patterns for bathroom or kitchen, decorative wall panels for indoors or out, and many more).
When decorating earthenware you can lay on paint rather more thickly; there is less risk of it flaking.

Firing

730°C for all earthenware.
800° to 830°C for industrial tiles, whose glaze will stand up to this temperature well. The colours will come out more glossy but less vibrant than at 730°C.
But red shades must *never* be fired at more than 730°C.

Scraped-out design on a white tile base, from India.

Detail of the Harlequin Mirror *by Marie-Thérèse Masias (see page 53).*

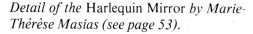

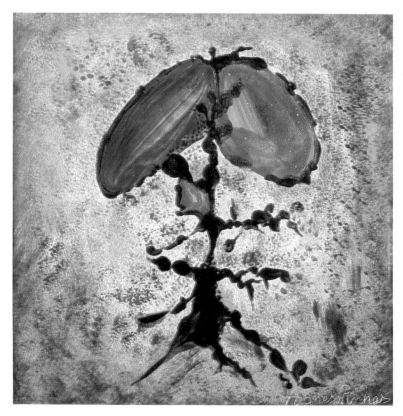

Design by Agnès Pinhas.

51

Delft tile, from the latter half of the 17th century.

Fireplace tiles, from the end of the 16th century.

Taken on Agfachrome. Musée Plantin-Moretus, Anvers (Belgium).

Harlequin mirror

A mirror frame of tiles, in two firings

First firing

Broad areas of colour.
Texture effects.
Clear patches to be left.
Patterns scratched with nib.
Brush lines.
The edges of the tiles painted.
The tiles numbered.

Second firing

Finishing the paintwork.
Going over it with wash-tints to match up the colour values.

Small earthenware tiles. Design by Marie-Thérèse Masias.

Place des Vosges (Vosges Square)

Decorative panel made up of fifteen tiles.
Produced in four firings.
Size: 75 × 45 cm.

Design by Agnès Pinhas.
Picture Joseph Sabbah.

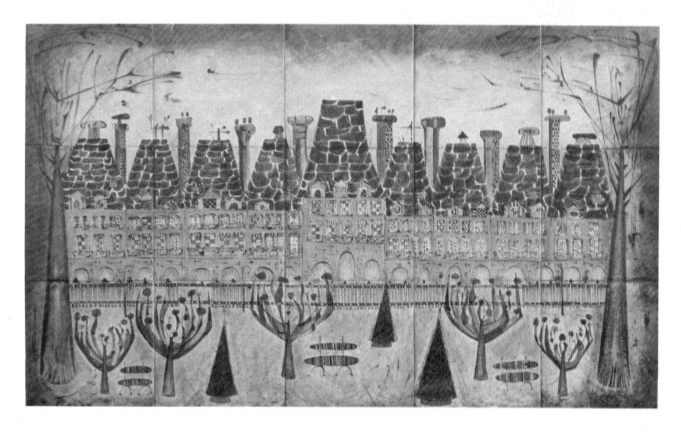

Imari porcelain from Japan, 17th century. Musées Nationaux picture.

History

Beginning, appropriately enough, in China, our history of ceramics is something of a lightning tour—it is, after all, an enormous subject for a small book like this!

The sophisticated culture of China has, through the ages, given birth to many unparalleled master craftsmen, true creators whose constantly evolving skills raised ceramics to the level of high art.

At the same time Japan, the Middle East civilizations and the Islamic culture that came after them also made great contributions to its development.

B.C.

China	
2698	Han dynasty annals already mention a superintendent of potteries.
2255	Canton area—Chun, a potter, crowned emperor.
2000 approx.	Potters' wheel (hand) first used. White tomb ware in very fine clay (kaolin?) found in An'yang excavations.
1300	Yang-chao: painted pottery, with engobe.
900-700	Lung-chan: grey, red, black, sometimes white pottery.
200	Development of high-temperature firing technique under natural cinder-grit cover.
185-206	Sin-Ping area, under Han dynasty—'proto-porcelain' (hard white impervious paste). Name *kaolin* probably derived from Kao-ling hill, near Peking, where china clay mined, also feldspar or petunze (similar to Cornish clay).

Middle East, Japan, Europe etc.	
3000 approx.	Jomon pottery, corded pattern (impressions and incisions).
2600	Mesopotamia—Babylon built (glazed bricks).
2500	Egypt—first kiln-fired pottery. Japan—Haniwa tomb figurines. Peru—Chavin: carved or engraved design, then rebated (till 2nd century AD).
1900	Egypt—Thebes, catacomb mural of potters kneading, shaping, firing pots.
1200	Greece—invention of the foot-wheel.
550	Persia—Susa: Archers Frieze, glazed brick.
200	Peru—Nazca: Very beautiful pottery with polychrome symbolic designs.
57	Korea: vitrified stoneware.
27	Japan: heavy Chinese influence transmitted by a Korean settlement which imports new techniques—establishment of a 'proto-porcelain' factory from China.

A.D.

375 — Nanking—building of a three-floored tower of glazed porcelain.

583 — Chin dynasty. Creation of the King-te-chin works for the emperor's own use. Use of kaolin and feldspar.

7th century — Tang dynasty—appearance of true porcelain 'blue as rainwashed sky'—special commission for the emperor. The secret, unfortunately, lost.

Throughout Asia and the Middle East many great centres were soon producing beautiful earthenware, a technique brought to Europe from North Africa by the Arab invasions. Muslim culture briefly dominant from Valencia to Peking.

5th century — Peru—Mochicha: carved design, sober century colours. One of the best Precolumbian wares.

8th to 10th centuries — Persia: relief or embossed design on light clay, with lead-based glaze usually green or yellow. Metallic oxides used. Egypt: Light clay, moulded design; green, brown, violet lead-based glaze.

10th to 15th centuries — Brazil: Marajo. Geometrical designs on white ground.

From the 9th century onwards, porcelain and earthenware developed together.

9th century — Sung dynasty: full development and apotheosis. Very beautiful wares: Ting (continued under Yuan) and crackle-glazed celadon ware—King-te-chin becomes a royal factory (for 8 centuries) using nearly 3000 kilns.

9th to 12th centuries — Mesopotamia, Egypt and Persia, Turkestan, Spain and Algeria: use of monochrome and polychrome lustres on tin-based glaze ground.

Engobe ceramic wall panelling, under-glaze decorations, polychrome on a white background,
1.50 × 1.72 metres. From Isfahan. Iran, early 17th century.
Musée de Louvre. Musées Nationaux picture.

Chinese covered vase, green family, reign of K'ang-Hsi (Ch'ing dynasty). Musée Dubouche, Limoges. Musées Nationaux picture.

13th century	Yuan: moulded relief designs (magnificent series of plates and platters in many museums).	1171	Mesopotamia—Saladin I sends 40-piece service of Chinese porcelain to caliph of Syria.
13th century	Mongol invasion of China. First designs painted on freely with brush.	12th century	Persia: white pottery, 'black silhouette' design, black engobe Spain: Paterna (tin mines) active centre for true earthenware, under the influence of craftsmen from Iran. Decoration on tin-based glaze. Almeria, Murcia, Malaga—pottery gilded with lustres, 'obra dorada', widely exported.
1271	Early European visitor Marco Polo arrives in China. He stays 16 years.		
1295	After a long journey home he brings back porcelains which arouse admiration and envy of European royalty. In his memoirs, sensational in Europe, he explains how porcelain is made.	1280	Granada: the Alhambra built, decorated with painted earthenware tiles called *azulejos*.
13th to 14th centuries	Golden age of Chinese porcelain, many innovations. Exported all over the world, now infatuated with it, it arouses great interest among collectors.	1320	Spain: Malaga—vases of the Alhambra.

*Three albarelli, Faenza majolica ware
from about 1580.
Musée de Cluny.
Musées Nationaux picture.*

14th to 18th centuries	Ming period (1368–1644), era of great prosperity, but forms were becoming heavy. Floral or symbolic motifs. Landmark in porcelain decoration: use of cobalt blue, imported from Iran. Beautifully transparent material, owing to King-te-chin kaolin. Rich red glaze derived from copper.

After the Ming period Chinese porcelain lost its special qualities as quickly as its success grew.
Material became thin, with a less rich glaze.
Colours were less harmonious, more clashing.
Shapes and designs became more complex.

18th to 20th centuries	Ch'ing dynasty: Three Heroes porcelain. Green family. Reign of Ch'ien Lung: end of blues and whites, complexity of motifs. Political collapse and fading reputation.

1442	Writer records that the beautiful earthenware made in Majorca, Spain, is very popular in Italy under the name *Majolica*. It would have been Spanish or Arab craftsmen who imported the methods of manufacturing earthenware with a tin-based glaze.

Earthenware

Spanish-Moorish earthenware and Italian *majolica* are the origin of all European earthenware.

16th century	Italy: Lead glazes rediscovered by Luca Della Robbia.
16th century	Italy: Hard-fire design. Production of pictures on earthenware with great skill. Principal creative centres: Florence, Faenza, then Pessaro, Urbino, Deruta, Venice, Padua, etc. At the same time soft blue porcelain was being made, also at Florence, for the Medici court; its secret was jealously guarded. Germany: Factories making glazed terracotta are famous, especially Hirschvogel's, at Nuremberg. Stoves are clad in ceramic tiles. Stoneware pots at Ratisbon, Bayreuth, etc.

Panel of Delft earthenware tiles, around 1670, perhaps from the porcelain Trianon at Versailles.
Hard-fire earthenware. 1.70 metres tall.
Musée de Sèvres. Musées Nationaux picture.

Low Countries	Delft: earthenware made here since 1310; painters are interested in its manufacture and paint beautiful ceramic plaques.
Britain	Difficult to date introduction of earthenware to Britain—1640, first salt-glazed stoneware. Burslem: Josiah Wedgwood (1730–1795), experimented with imitation of precious stones; produced cream-coloured pieces in fine stoneware, called 'Queen's Ware'. Specialist in busts and statues, and inventor of the pyrometer, he gave a great boost to Britain's ceramics industry. Factories at Etruria (Stoke-on-Trent), Liverpool, Bristol. Josiah Spode (1754–1827) developed stone china, porcelain and bone china; he popularised the 'willow pattern'.

Central Europe—Hungary (Tata)	
France	Many Italians settle at Lyons and Nevers, there founding the first earthenware factories. They train the French masters of Rouen, Nimes, Montpellier. Also: Guido Andries settled in Anvers around 1510 where he also trained followers; Spanish craftsmen had been arriving since the 16th century.
Japan	Arrival of Korean potters, prisoners of war who settle at Arita, near the port of Imari. They make blue and white porcelain. The potter Sakaido makes the first designs under cobalt blue glaze (Iranian discovery).
1508–18	Portuguese import Japanese porcelain into Europe.
1539	Bernard Palissy, glazier of Saintes, begins experiments to rediscover the formula of the glaze of a majolica cup which has impressed him. Unshakeable determination but a whole art to learn. He goes from disappointment to disappointment until one day he fires his glazes in a glassmaker's furnace; the beginning of his successes. He builds himself a kiln and fires material for 6 days and 6 nights. Only after 15 or 16 years does he find the glaze formula he seeks. He calls his pottery *rustiques figulines*, country ware, and rediscovers the art of glazing earthenware, still unknown in France.
1555	The Dutch East India Company sends an agent to Canton to penetrate the mysteries of porcelain manufacture, but he returns baffled.

17th century
Still great production, but with no vitality now, of earthenware in Mediterranean Europe (Spain, Portugal, Italy); more spirit in the north, at Delft in the Low Countries and Nevers in France.

Two great stylistic trends:
Classical, inspired by the Italian renaissance;
Oriental, because of the massive shipments of porcelain from China and Japan. Polychrome decoration, floral wall panels.

Rouen, France, also comes under this influence.
Also benefits from a 50-year manufacturing permit granted to Nicholas Poirel and then Edmée Poterat.

Maclou Abasquesne experiments and produces earthenware tiles for decorating the Chateau d'Ecouen.

Rouen style: radiant blue in imitation of Chinese ware.

18th century
Delft—production becomes more ordinary and especially so in the wares made specially for France (French Delft or *'paysans orangistes'.)*

In the 18th century, French taste characterizes European earthenware production. From the mid-century on decoration is by slow-fire process in all factories.

Jasmine cup and saucer with fluted base and silver-gilt handle, in hard porcelain. The medallion is a portrait of the empress Marie-Louise by Mme. Jaquotot (after Isabey).
Musée de Sèvres. Musées Nationaux picture.

Porcelain in Europe

In China the secret of porcelain manufacture was well kept, and this provoked constant interest and envy.

Many attempts, official and otherwise, were made to try to break this silence, but in vain. All the kings and princes of European courts dreamed of one day establishing their own factories and there making a porcelain as beautiful as that brought back from the East; many of them set up laboratories and hired researchers to investigate the problem.

Earliest attempts

1673—Rouen, by Louis Poterat.

1707—In Germany the Elector of Saxony establishes the alchemist Böttger in a castle-cum-laboratory to continue his research into porcelain.

1709—Böttger recognises the white powder he uses on his wigs as the famous kaolin, mined at Aüe near Schneeberg; his tests prove positive.

1710—Albert castle becomes a factory making the first hard porcelain (fired at high temperatures and unmarkable by steel). In 1712 it is christened Saxony porcelain. The secret is jealously guarded.

1712—following this, great excitement in Europe among the crowned heads and the researchers.

Then, when letters arrive from d'Entrecolles, the Jesuit missionary to China, describing the manufacture of porcelain, there is a massive growth of interest; ingredients are shipped from China, but cannot be identified in their powdered form.

1718—Saxon emigrés make it possible to open porcelain production at Vienna in Austria.

At Chelsea in England a soft phosphatic porcelain is made, soon to become an enormously popular hybrid porcelain, so much so that hard porcelain is never manufactured there.

At Doccia, Italy, the marquis Ginori imports feldspar and kaolin from China, invites noted chemists, artists and designers and makes a beautiful porcelain imitating the Chinese product.

1736—Capodimonte, Italy. Had the king of the Two Sicilies got hold of the 'Meissen[1] secret'? Certainly he sponsors the production of one of the most beautiful European porcelains.

1738—Vincennes, France. A laboratory is installed in the Chateau for the Dubois brothers from Chantilly, who discover nothing. Their successor Gavrant makes a soft porcelain, and disposes of his rights to Orry de Fulvy and Adams, who, with Boileau, makes this factory extremely prosperous. At the recommendation of Mme. de Pompadour in 1756 it becomes the Manufacture Royale de Sèvres (whose lovely products will dominate Europe for a long time to come).

There research into making hard porcelain continues.

1759—Charles III, king of the Two Sicilies, becomes king of Spain and moves his Capodimonte workers to Buen Retiro near Madrid (destroyed in 1812).

1768—Discovery of a kaolin and feldspar bed at Saint Yriex near Limoges.

1771—A factory patronized by the Comte d'Artois is opened in the old Massie earthenware factory at Limoges.

60 years later Limoges becomes the centre of the French porcelain industry, with thirty factories, which are greatly boosted in 1842 when the Havilland factory begins to export massive amounts of its beautiful wares to the USA.

At present manual decoration has almost totally disappeared, to be replaced by chromolithography (designs being put onto the pieces by *decalcomanies*, transfers printed from lithographic stone—hence the name).

The process still needs a decorator to create the initial pattern, however.

1776—Scandinavia also begins to manufacture porcelain exactly like that from China, having first made soft paste: Copenhagen (Denmark), Marieberg (Sweden) and also St. Petersburg in Russia.

1812—Sèvres enjoys great prestige under the 47-year directorship of M. Brongniart.

National, royal and imperial commissions are carried out.

A speciality is developed—Sèvres Blue (3 layers of cobalt blue superimposed with a stencil and fired at 940°C).

Later, under the direction of Carrier-Belleuse and de Sandier, it invites the collaboration of artists of the stature of Guimard and Rodin. As it does today, with Hadju, Penalba, Arp, Zao-wou-Ki, Agam, Calder, Guittet, and others; their creations only represent 10% of the factory's total output, mostly devoted to reproducing old designs on old forms. Marking of pieces has been introduced to fight off imitators. The current mark was created by the painter Mathieu in 1970.

Bali, design by Roch Popelier on porcelain by Georges Boyer, Limoges. Picture Manfred Seelow.

19th century

A new enthusiasm spread from England, inspired by Ruskin and Morris, favouring the decorative arts as a calling in reaction against industrial civilization. This side of the arts prominent at international expositions and fairs; Beauty and Craftsmanship would henceforth be associated, also as a stimulus to encourage people to work in the crafts field. Opening of specialized museums in European cities. Art Nouveau, Jugendstil, Liberty and Modern Style bring great prestige to design.

At the turn of the century, economic trends do not favour the ceramics industry, especially earthenware (crisis of 1885). But in 1907 André Mathey opens his Asnières studio to painter friends whom he introduces to polychrome decoration over tin-based glaze, among them are Odilon Redon, Renoir, M. Denis, Bonnard, Rouault, Vlaminck, Van Dongen, etc. They take part in exhibitions.

End of 19th to early 20th century

Many ceramicists rise to prominence and advance the craft.
Tiffany: America, France.
J. Hoffmann: Germany.
Van der Velde: Belgium.
Juriaankok: Holland.
Ruskin and Moore: Britain.
Peyrusson, Delaherche, Dammouse, Chaplet, among others in France.

At Vallauris Picasso also turns to decorating forms he creates for himself; he revives Vallauris' operations through the interest aroused by his astonishing creations.

In 1919 the Bauhaus school in German rethink the aesthetics of forms, then create for the German ceramics industry, upon which the influence of their 'white porcelain' is still evident today.

The Scandinavians, and in particular the Finns, also set out to purify form, and their decoration achieves high standards; they are helped by industrial concerns such as Arabia, which allows interested artists to make single pieces or series in conditions ideal for experiment. Rosenthal-Studio-Linie in Germany follows an almost similar policy, for the production of pieces in series, but to a high standard.

For the craftsman, often very much on his own, professional associations and Arts and Crafts societies offer the chance of group exhibitions and meeting other practitioners—always fruitful—and an aware audience.

It seems, happily, that people today are attaching increasing importance to the quality of life, and they like to surround themselves with beautiful things, preferably handmade. Many young people will reach out to the craftsman, and so are sometimes inspired to take up the craft themselves and appreciate it all the more. Let us hope that this popular goodwill will shortly bring a new and lasting breath of life to arts and crafts, and to the ceramic arts in particular.

Some contemporary ceramic artists

Figures from Eastern fairy-tales.
Designs by Bjorn Wiinblad.
Picture Rosenthal.

Rosenthal-Studio-Linie

Germany

The Rosenthal studio was set up around 1950.

Its policy is to entrust certain artists and designers—chosen through a panel of international art experts—with the creation of the Rosenthal line and establishing the style of their day.

We would be glad if more countries were inspired by this generous and effective policy towards art and artists.

Sonia Delaunay

France

'Nothing is done by chance, and everything is done with love.'
Wife of painter Robert Delaunay, whose studies of colour she has shared while following her own creative paths, above all those which led her to porcelain decoration.
Polychrome design on hard Limoges porcelain. Fired at 1400°C.

Carnival *and* Yellow Dancer, *by Sonia Delaunay.*
Artcurial Edition.
Picture Artcurial.

Bjorn Wiinblad

Copenhagen—Denmark

An accomplished artist whose work is rich with invention and technical innovations; it includes theatre set and costume design, book illustrations, tapestry and ceramics.

His vast output in this field demonstrates an exceptional mastery of it.

Picture Lennard, Copenhagen.

Denise Parouty

France

Porcelain painter, from Périgueux.

Trained at École des Arts Décoratifs, Limoges.

Has taken part in many exhibitions.

Her creations reflect the everyday world, but seen through her inner world, realities or dreams.

These creations are inspired by nature, to which she feels very close: trees, leaves, flowers, birds, various animals and personages. Some symbolize the pattern of the seasons.

The essence of being an artist or a craftsman is knowing how to work with spirit, heart and hands.

Elves and Shepherds.

Sky paths. *Hard-fire design using oxides, 1400°C; 45 × 35cm.*

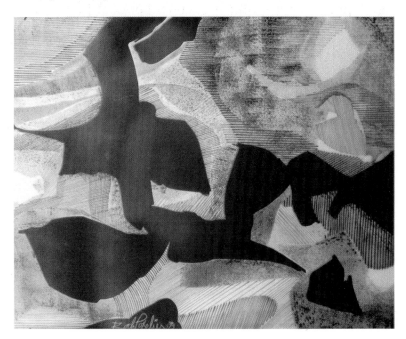

Roch Popelier

France

Ceramic artist, decorator and designer.
Training: École des Arts Décoratifs, Limoges.
Many exhibitions in France and abroad.
Well-known and appreciated designer at Limoges.
Hand-drawn design under glaze, high heat on porcelain.
Creator of design prototypes for the porcelain industry, and of carpet designs for Aubusson and Paris.

Agnès Pinhas-Massin

France

Porcelain and earthenware painter.
Training: École des Métiers d'Art, Arts appliqués, Paris.
Member of the Maison des Métiers d'Art Français.
Has taken part in many exhibitions.
Designs and paints by hand soft-fire decoration on china.
Decorative panels, engravings, lithographs, figurines, illustrations.
Whether a piece is decorative or just useful, it is the result either of an intense impulse or, more often, of slow and painstaking studies of rhythms, colours, materials and designs.
Her creations are inspired by the animal world, by the beauty of plants and from the imagination. They allow her to merge her craft with her life, to communicate with others and to love them.

Flute player.
Slow-fire on earthenware.

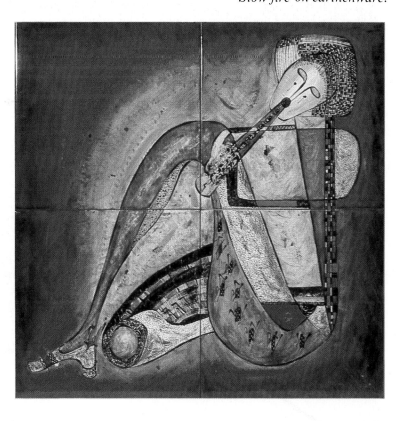

Louis-Robert Mallet

France

Porcelain painter: illustrator.
He has worked for many studios.
Many exhibitions in France and abroad.
As well as soft-fire porcelain painting, he creates transfer designs for mass-produced porcelain, and illustrates books and other publications.
His work on porcelain is absolutely remarkable.
He is always seeking out new subjects, which he expresses through very elaborate design and composition.

Roots.
Study in textures.
Porcelain, soft-fire.

Monique Saint-Marc

France

Porcelain painter at Limoges.
Training: four years at the École des Arts Décoratifs.
Divides her activities between the factory and her own work, which takes its inspiration from nature: animals, flowers. . . .

One of the designs for a fish service.